AQA STUDY GUIDE

GCSE 9–1

UNSEEN POETRY

SCHOLASTIC

Author Richard Durant and Cindy Torn

Reviewer Rob Pollard

Editorial team Rachel Morgan, Audrey Stokes, Lesley Densham, Kate Pedlar

Typesetting Jayne Rawlings/Oxford Raw Design

Cover design Dipa Mistry and Jason Cox

App development Hannah Barnett, Phil Crothers and RAIOSOFT International Pvt Ltd

Photographs
page 12: eagle perched on rock, Crystal Kirk/Shutterstock; page 16: eagle's stare, dtfrancis15/Shutterstock; page 20: hanging bat, BOONCHUAY PROMJIAM/Shutterstock; page 22: girl sitting exam, Monkey Business Images/Shutterstock; page 26: wood burning, designelements/Shutterstock; green fern leaf, ND700/Shutterstock; page 28: robin, Ger Bosma Photos/Shutterstock; page 30: rainbow, designelements/Shutterstock; page 33: dark, deserted room, Kim Wutimet/Shutterstock; page 37: eggs in wire basket, Julsmark/Shutterstock; page 40: cloudy sky, KC Lens and Footage/Shutterstock; page 45: mop and bucket, Skylines/Shutterstock; page 48: woman playing piano, Morphart Creation/Shutterstock; page 52: grand piano, sukiyaki/Shutterstock; page 54: overripe fruit, Dan Hanscom/Shutterstock

Published in the UK by Scholastic Education, 2019
Scholastic Education, Scholastic Distribution Centre, Bosworth Avenue, Tournament Fields, Warwick, CV34 6UQ
Scholastic Ireland, 89E Lagan Road, Dublin Industrial Estate, Glasnevin, Dublin, D11 HP5F

A CIP catalogue record for this book is available from the British Library.
ISBN 978-1407-18322-0

Printed and bound by Leo Paper Products Ltd, China

This book is made of materials from well-managed, FSC®-certified forests and other controlled sources.

MIX
Paper | Supporting responsible forestry
FSC
www.fsc.org   FSC® C020056

Designed using Adobe InDesign

Acknowledgements
The publishers gratefully acknowledge permission to reproduce the following copyright material: **Bloodaxe Books** for 'Living Space' by Imitiaz Dharker from *Postcards from God* by Imitiaz Dharker, (Bloodaxe Books, 1997); **David Higham Associates** for 'My Grandmother' by Elizabeth Jennings from *The Collected Poems* by Elizabeth Jennings, (Carcanet Press, 2012); **Frances Crofts Cornford Will Trust** for 'Childhood' by Frances Cornford from *Selected Poems* by Frances Cornford, (Enitharmon Press, 1996); **Little, Brown Book Group** for 'Woman Work' by Maya Angelou from *And Still I Rise* by Maya Angelou, (Virago Press, 2013); **Peepal Tree Press** for 'In between days' by Raman Mundair from *Lovers, Liars, Conjurers and Thieves* by Raman Mundair, (Peepal Tree Press, 2003); **Penguin Random House** for 'The Playhouse Key' by Rachel Field from *Taxis and toadstools* by Rachel Field, (World's Work, 1962). **Rogers, Coleridge and White** for 'Catrin' by Gillian Clarke from *Selected Poems* by Gillian Clarke, (Picador, 2016); **Family of Vernon Scannell** for 'Nettles' by Vernon Scannell from *GCSE Poetry Anthology: Moon on the Tides* by AQA, (Oxford University Press, 2010)

Every effort has been made to trace copyright holders for the works reproduced in this book, and the publishers apologise for any inadvertent omissions.

Note from the publisher:
Please use this product in conjunction with the official specification and sample assessment materials. Ask your teacher if you are unsure where to find them.

Contents

Check your answers on the free revision app or at www.scholastic.co.uk/gcse

How to use this book

This Study Guide is designed to help you prepare effectively for your **AQA GCSE English literature** exam questions on Unseen poetry (Paper 2, Section C).

The content has been organised in three sections. It starts with focusing on how to approach the exam questions and what the examiner is looking for, before moving on to example pairs of poems and finally practice AQA exam-style questions.

HOW TO REVISE!

The basics

1 The first section of this book provides guidance on how to approach each of the two Unseen poetry questions using a flexible set of prompts in the form of a 'response framework'. This framework will support your understanding of each of the poems you are presented with in the exam by encouraging you to look at them from a number of different points of view.

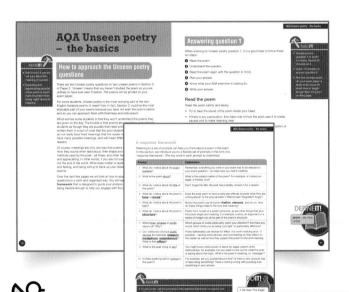

This section also guides you through the process of understanding each question, and planning and writing answers to ensure that you meet your AQA examiner's expectations.

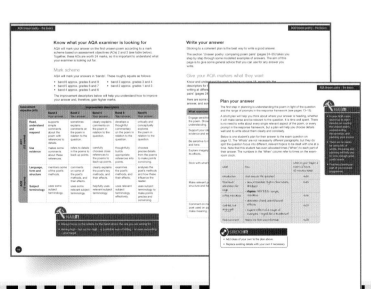

Comparing poem pairs

2 In the second section, we model how to work through example exam questions using pairs of poems. This section also provides AQA exam-style questions for you to answer yourself. This will help you understand how to write a good answer to the questions in your exam. Additional activities are provided for you to work through and practise.

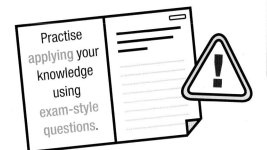

Practise applying your knowledge using exam-style questions.

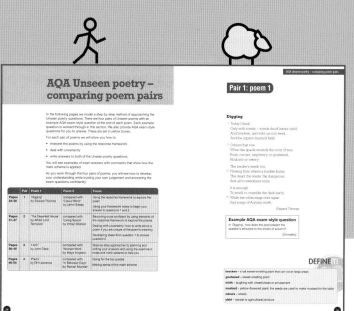

Practice questions

3 Finally, you will find an extended 'AQA exam-style questions' section for you to work through applying the skills you have acquired.

Stick to the
TIME LIMITS
you will need to in the exam.

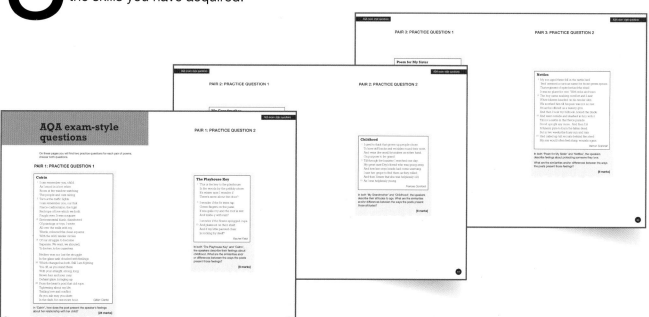

Features of this guide

The best way to retain information is to take an active approach to revision.

Throughout this book, you will find lots of features that will make your revision an active, successful process.

SNAPIT!

Use the Snap it! feature in the revision app to take pictures of key concepts and information. Great for revision on the go!

DEFINEIT!

Explains the meaning of difficult words from the poems.

Callouts Additional explanations of important points.

Words shown in **purple bold** can be found in the glossary on page 64.

Find methods of relaxation that work for you throughout the revision period.

Regular exercise helps stimulate the brain and will help you relax.

DOIT!

Activities to embed your knowledge and understanding and prepare you for the exam.

NAILIT!

Succinct and vital tips on how to do well in your exam.

STRETCHIT!

Provides content that stretches you further.

REVIEWIT!

Helps you to consolidate and understand what you have learned before moving on.

Revise in pairs or small groups and deliver presentations on topics to each other.

FOR HIGH-MARK QUESTIONS, SPEND TIME **PLANNING** YOUR ANSWER!

AQA exam-style question

AQA exam-style sample questions based on the poems shown are given on some pages. Use the sample mark schemes on pages 18 and 21 to help you assess your responses. This will also help you understand what you could do to improve your response.

- The **free revision app** can be downloaded to your mobile phone (iOS and Android), making **on-the-go revision** easy.

- Use the revision calendar to help map out your revision in the lead-up to the exam.

- Complete multiple-choice questions and create your own SNAP IT revision cards.

www.scholastic.co.uk/gcse

Online answers and additional resources
All of the tasks in this book are designed to get you thinking and to consolidate your understanding through thought and application. Therefore, it is important to write your own answers before checking. Use a separate piece of paper so that you can draft your response and work out the best way of answering.
Online you will find a copy of each poem with detailed annotations. Do not look at those until you have explored the poem thoroughly for yourself.

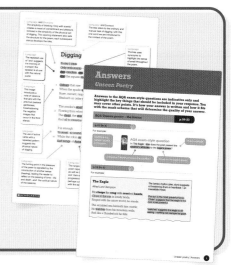

Get plenty of sleep, especially the night before an exam.

LOOK AFTER YOURSELF

Help your brain by looking after your whole body!

Once you have worked through a section, you can check your answers to Do it!, Stretch it! and the exam practice sections on the app or at **www.scholastic.co.uk/gcse**. Annotated poems are available at **www.scholastic.co.uk/gcse-poetry**.

An introduction to your AQA Unseen poetry

Why study Unseen poetry?

Even before you ever read poetry, you will have responded to songs and their lyrics from an early age. Poetry has been used throughout history to explore the world around us and to examine people's lives and thoughts. This section of your two literature exam papers is where you can use all of your creativity to respond to the poems in front of you.

What is the aim of the Unseen poetry section of the exam?

The aim of this section is to allow you to explain your understanding of poems that you have never seen before and to be able to make connections as you read.

If we wish to grow as people who can learn from what other people have been through, through a whole range of situations, we can learn from the varied experiences these poets bring us.

Unseen poetry in your AQA exam

Unseen poetry is examined in Section C (the third section) of your second AQA GCSE English Literature exam, Paper 2 Modern Texts and Poetry. Here is how it fits into the overall English literature exam framework:

Paper 1 Time: **1 hour 45 minutes**	**Paper 2** Time: **2 hours 15 minutes**
Section A: Shakespeare	Section A: Modern prose or drama
Section B: 19th-century novel	Section B: Poetry anthology
	Section C: Unseen poetry

There will be **two questions** on Unseen poetry and you will be presented with two unseen poems. You must answer **both** questions. You should spend **50 minutes** planning and writing your answers to the questions. There are 32 marks available for the Unseen poetry questions: question 1 has 24 marks available and question 2 has eight marks.

The **first** Unseen poetry question will come with a copy of the poem printed on your exam paper. You will find the question just after the poem. The question will ask you to analyse a theme from the given poem. The **second** Unseen poetry question will develop the theme from the first question. You will be given a second poem and you will compare the way the two poets develop this chosen theme. You must answer both questions.

What do examiners want to see in your responses to the Unseen poetry questions?

✓ Your engagement with and understanding of the poems.

✓ Your responses supported by credible evidence.

✓ Your exploration of imagery.

✓ Your sensitivity to mood and tone.

✓ Your *relevant* points on structure and form.

✓ Your comments on things the writer did on purpose to make their meaning clear.

✓ Your focus on the poets' 'ways' as outlined in the question; possible 'ways' (methods) could include:

- the creation of a **mood/tone**, **perspective/voice**
- the use/effect of particular **word choices**
- the use/effect of description including **imagery**
- **structural elements**
- **titles**
- **sound patterning**
- **tense**
- **punctuation**.

What do examiners want you to avoid?

✗ Vague speculation about an author's autobiographical details.

✗ Writing about the theme in general (for example, aging) without referring to how it is treated in the poem.

✗ Spotting features without discussing their effect.

Finally…

Always remember to **answer the question** on your paper!

Make sure you understand what the question is asking.

How to approach the Unseen poetry questions

There are two Unseen poetry questions on two unseen poems in Section C of Paper 2. 'Unseen' means that you haven't studied the poem so you are unlikely to have ever seen it before. The poems will be printed on your exam paper.

For some students, Unseen poetry is the most worrying part of the two English literature exams. It needn't be. In fact, Section C could be the most enjoyable part of your exams because you have not seen the poems before and so you can approach them with freshness and enthusiasm.

What worries some students is that they won't understand the poems they are given on the day. The trouble is that poems are sometimes presented to students as though they are puzzles that need solving, as though the poet has written them in a sort of code that the poor student has to crack. But poems do not really have fixed meanings that the reader must get right. Most poems have many possible meanings, and will mean different things to different readers.

Of course, meanings are only one way that poems can engage readers. How they sound when read aloud, their shape and **form**, images and other methods used by the poet – all these, and other features, are worth noticing and appreciating. In other words, if you are not sure what a poem *means*, it's not the end of the world. What does matter is reading carefully with thought and feeling, and being willing to back up your ideas with evidence from the poems.

Over the next few pages we will look at how to approach the Unseen poetry questions in a calm and organised way. You will learn about a **response framework** that is designed to guide your analysis of the poems while also being flexible enough to help you engage with the poems in your own way.

Answering question 1

When working on Unseen poetry question 1, it is a good idea to follow these six steps:

1 Read the poem.

2 Understand the question.

3 Read the poem again with the question in mind.

4 Plan your answer.

5 Know what your AQA examiner is looking for.

6 Write your answer.

Read the poem

Read the poem calmly and slowly.

- Try to hear the sound of the poem inside your head.

- If there is any punctuation, then take note of how the poet uses it to create pauses and to make meaning clear.

- Notice what the poem is *about*. For example, 'The Eagle' is a description of an eagle, concentrating on the bird's power.

Read the poem, 'The Eagle' shown below.

NAILIT!

- Unseen poetry question 1 is worth 24 marks. Spend 35 minutes on it.

- Leave 15 minutes to answer question 2.

- The first unseen poem on your exam paper is likely to be about 20 short lines in length (longer than the poem on this page).

The Eagle

1 He clasps the crag with crooked hands;
   Close to the sun in lonely lands,
   Ringed with the azure world, he stands.

   The wrinkled sea beneath him crawls;
5 He watches from his mountain walls,
   And like a thunderbolt he falls.

Alfred Lord Tennyson

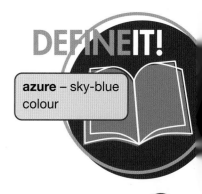

DEFINEIT!

azure – sky-blue colour

DO IT!

Here is another exam question on 'The Eagle'. Prepare it in the same way as on the right.

In 'The Eagle', how does the poet present the speaker's attitudes to the eagle's power?

DO IT!

Add a couple more notes to the annotations on the right. Stay relevant to the poem and the question focus.

Understand the question

Make sure you understand the exam question so that you do not include in your answer material that is irrelevant to what the question has asked.

Below is an AQA exam-style question. The question has been prepared by a student so that they fully understand it. Look at their notes.

AQA exam-style question

In 'The Eagle', how does the poet present the speaker's feelings about the eagle?

Poet's methods

Underline key, relevant details in the poem.

Strength/power/admiration/fear?

Focus on the eagle.

Read the poem again with the question in mind

Now that you have an idea of what the poem is about, and you know what the exam question is asking, read the poem through again.

Look at how a student has annotated 'The Eagle' with particular attention to the key words in the exam question:

Key to highlighting

Tennyson's attitudes

His methods

The eagle's power

The Eagle

He clasps the crag with crooked hands;
Close to the sun in lonely lands,
Ringed with the azure world, he stands.

The wrinkled sea beneath him crawls;
He watches from his mountain walls,
And like a thunderbolt he falls.

'The Eagle' not 'An...' makes it special/Tennyson is in awe of eagle?

Hard 'c' alliteration

Same rhyme for each line: authoritative/eagle is boss crawls/beneath...suggests worship?

All-seeing/watches from on high - like a god?

Thunderbolt - also god? Lethal!

The notes made by this student took perhaps 90 seconds, but they provide nearly enough material to develop into a whole, relevant answer.

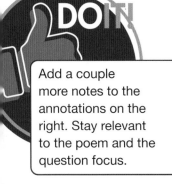

12

A response framework

Referring to a set of prompts can help you think about a poem in the exam.
In this section, we introduce you to a flexible set of prompts in the form of a
'response framework'. (The key word in each prompt is underlined.)

Prompt	Explanation
1 What do I notice about the <u>exam question</u>?	Remember, everything you write in your exam has to be relevant to your exam question – so make sure you read it carefully.
2 What is the poem <u>about</u>?	What is the subject matter of the poem? For example, is it about an eagle, a holiday, love?
3 What do I notice about the <u>title</u> of the poem?	Don't forget the title: the poet has probably chosen it for a reason.
4 What do I notice about the poem's **tone** or **mood**?	Does the poet seem to have a particular attitude towards what they are writing about? Is the tone sarcastic? Affectionate? Regretful? Angry?
5 What do I notice about the poem's <u>form</u>?	Notice the poet's use of rhyme, **rhythm**, **stanzas**, and so on. How do these things relate to the tone and meaning?
6 What do I notice about the poem's **structure**?	Poetic form is part of a poem's structure, as are other things that give the poem shape and meaning. For example, a story, an argument or a series of images can all be part of the poem's structure.
7 Which <u>lines</u>, <u>phrases</u> or <u>words</u> stand out? Why?	Which groups of words particularly catch your attention? Are there any words which strike you as being 'just right' or particularly effective?
8 Do I notice any obvious <u>poetic devices</u> (for example, **imagery**, **metaphors**, **enjambment**)? What is their **effect**?	Poets deliberately use devices for effect. It is worth noticing and – if possible – naming some devices, and commenting on their effect on the reader as well as how they support the poem's tone and meaning.
9 What is the poet trying to <u>say</u>?	You might know what a poem is about (an eagle, parent–child relationships, for example), but you need to look out for what the poet is saying about that topic. What is the poem's meaning, or 'message'?
10 Is there anything odd or <u>curious</u> in the poem?	For example, are you puzzled about a line? Is there a very unusual way of describing something? There is nothing wrong with puzzling over something in your answer.

NAILIT!

- In your exam, use the prompts in the response framework to support your understanding of the poem.

- Even though you won't have time in your exam to write down your answers to each prompt, use the full response framework in the early stages of your revision to get yourself used to looking at any poem from a number of points of view.

- As your exam approaches, adjust your use of the framework in light of the exam time pressures.

DOIT!

- Re-read 'The Eagle'. Keep the exam question in mind.

- Try to answer the prompts in the response framework. (Each question is covered later in this section, but first try to answer the questions yourself.)

A response framework example

The notes below are a very thorough example of the response framework in action, and they go into far more detail than you should attempt in your exam. However, the notes do indicate the *range* of comments you could make in your answer, and they prove that you could never be expected to say everything about a poem – even one as short as 'The Eagle'.

NAILIT!

You need to justify your ideas about a poem's meaning, but don't assume that a poem has hidden meanings: the poet might be trying to say something very straightforward.

1	What do I notice about the exam question?	The exam question asks how the poet presents the speaker's attitudes to the eagle's power, so I need to focus on the poet's methods and whether they are effective, how the speaker feels and responds towards the eagle, and how the eagle's power is portrayed.
2	What is the poem about?	'The Eagle' seems to be quite simply a description of an eagle. The description concentrates on the eagle as predator and on its power and determination. The poem expresses admiration for these qualities.
3	What do I notice about the title of the poem?	The title is very ordinary and factual compared with the powerful and sometimes threatening mood of the poem. We know from the title that the point of the poem is going to be something about an eagle. However, the title is '*The Eagle*', not '*An Eagle*'. This suggests the poem is about one particular eagle - or about the whole species, not about any eagle.
4	What do I notice about the poem's tone or mood?	The poem seems to have a mood of quiet threat. It makes us feel as though we are part of the eagle's prey. We feel small and powerless compared with the eagle high up on his perch. The tone suggests that the speaker admires the eagle. He is looking up to him in two senses.
5	What do I notice about the poem's form?	The poem's form is neat, consisting of two equal stanzas with an unusual **rhyme scheme** - each stanza has only one rhyme: '-ands', in stanza one; '-alls', in stanza two. The lines can be read with an even rhythm too: there are eight syllables and four **stresses** in each line: dee<u>dum</u>/dee<u>dum</u>/dee<u>dum</u>/dee<u>dum</u>/. For example, 'He <u>clasps</u> the <u>crag</u> with <u>crooked</u> <u>hands</u>.' The even, steady beat is like a slow drum, giving an ominous feel to the poem, building to the climax of the eagle's deadly dive.
6	What do I notice about the poem's structure?	The organisation or structure of the poem comes mainly from its form (see above). The poem also has dramatic tension, designed to hold our attention through to the end. The first stanza describes the eagle as a watchful hunter. The second stanza focuses on what he sees below and then on his sudden movement from where he standing was to where he was looking.

7	Which lines, phrases or words stand out? Why?	The first line stands out for me. The line is completely regular in its rhythm, alternating between unstressed and stressed syllables: dee<u>dum</u>, dee<u>dum</u>, dee<u>dum</u>, dee<u>dum</u>. You can feel this line 'pulsing' like a heartbeat, conveying the eagle's determination and concentration.
		I particularly like the phrase 'crooked hands'. 'Clenched' would have been just as good in some ways, but 'crooked' suggests something more dangerous, untrustworthy and ugly, and the word has a harsh, destructive sound like the word 'crag' just before it. Also, why 'hands' and not 'talons'? 'Hands' suggests the eagle is not just acting from instinct: it might be scheming and planning evil deeds - like a human can.
		I notice that most of the words are simple and ordinary so as not to make the eagle sound over-sophisticated and civilised: he is definitely a killer. For example, he 'falls' from his perch. This might suggest he has lost control, but here it probably suggests he is determined to reach the ground - and his prey - in the shortest possible time. Other simple word choices suggesting the eagle is completely confident about his power include 'stands' and 'clasps'. Tennyson's straightforward vocabulary expresses his admiration for the eagle's single-mindedness and complete power.
		'Ringed' stands out for a different reason. It is not an ordinary word choice such as 'surrounded', which would have implied there was something more powerful than the eagle, something that could limit his power. 'Ringed' suggests the eagle is being protected rather than confined. Also, a ring is a precious thing, perhaps suggesting the king-like status of the eagle in his world.
8	Do I notice any obvious poetic devices? What is their effect?	Device: **personification**
		The eagle has 'hands' rather than 'talons'. This makes the eagle human, perhaps suggesting that the eagle is a symbol of tyranny in the human world - the powerful preying on the weak. The fact that the world of the eagle is 'lonely' supports the personification: presumably a lone eagle would not feel lonely - only a human feels lonely.
		Device: **simile**
		The eagle falls 'like a thunderbolt'. This makes him sound god-like, the sort of god you find in ancient mythology - a god who seems to act in a frighteningly random and violent way.
		Device: **alliteration**
		The 'c' alliteration in the first line has a hard sound and helps to emphasise the toughness of the eagle.

NAILIT!

It is useful to be able to mention poetic devices by name. It saves time and shows your knowledge of subject terminology. However, simply naming devices is pointless: you need to consider their *effect* on the reader – how they make the reader think and feel – and how they support the poem's meaning.

| 9 | what is the poet trying to say? | The poet's intentions can be interpreted in different ways. Tennyson could be presenting the eagle as a terrifying, even evil, animal. We might even wonder if Tennyson is presenting the eagle as a symbol of God's power and anger, making 'The Eagle' a religious poem. |
| 10 | Is there anything odd or curious in the poem? | For example, why does Tennyson say that the eagle's habitat is a 'lonely' place? Does he simply mean that the eagle is a 'lone operator' (as we might say) or is he suggesting that the eagle is lonely, perhaps feeling excluded from the world he raids for food? |

Plan your answer

The first step in planning is understanding the poem in light of the question and the range of prompts in the response framework (see pages 13–16).

A short plan will help you think about where your answer is heading, whether it will make sense and be relevant to the question. It is time well spent. There is no need to write about every single relevant aspect of the poem, or every prompt in the response framework, but a plan will help you choose details well and to write about them clearly and concisely.

Below is one student's plan for their answer to the exam question on page 12. The 'Whats' are not necessarily different paragraphs, but they do split the question focus into different, relevant topics to be dealt with one at a time. Note that this student has even allocated times ('When') to each part of their answer. The numbers in the 'When' column refer to times on the exam-room clock.

What	How	When in your Paper 2 exam (2 hours 15 minutes total)
Introduction	Just answer the question!	10.33
Fear/awe/ admiration for eagle	• slow, irresistible rhythm (four beats, dee<u>dum</u>)	10.35
Lethal, merciless	• **rhyme** AAA BBB - simple, relentless	10.43
God-like, but angry god	• alliteration (hard, violent)/sound effects • explore effect of a couple of examples - 'ringed', 'like a thunderbolt'	10.51
Final comment	Makes me feel uncomfortable	10.58

 **STRETCHIT!**

- Add ideas of your own to the plan above.
- Replace existing details with your own if necessary.

Know what your AQA examiner is looking for

AQA will mark your answer on the first unseen poem according to a mark scheme based on assessment objectives (AOs) 2 and 3 (see table below). Together, these AOs are worth 24 marks, so it is important to understand what your examiner is looking out for.

Mark scheme

AQA will mark your answers in 'bands'. These roughly equate as follows:

- band 6 approx. grades 8 and 9
- band 5 approx. grades 6 and 7
- band 4 approx. grades 5 and 6
- band 3 approx. grades 3 and 4
- band 2 approx. grades 1 and 2.

The improvement descriptors below will help you understand how to improve your answer and, therefore, gain higher marks.

Assessment objective (AO)		Improvement descriptors				
		Band 2 Your answer…	**Band 3** Your answer…	**Band 4** Your answer…	**Band 5** Your answer…	**Band 6** Your answer…
AO1 (12 marks)	**Read, understand and respond**	supports simple comments about the poem with references to details.	sometimes explains comments on the poem in relation to the question.	clearly explains comments on the poem in relation to the question.	develops a thoughtful commentary on the poem in relation to the question.	critically and conceptually explores the poem in relation to the question.
	Use evidence	makes some comments about these references.	refers to details in the poems to back up points.	carefully chooses close references to the poems to back up points.	thoughtfully builds appropriate references into points.	chooses precise details from the poems to make points convincing.
AO2 (12 marks)	**Language, form and structure**	mentions some of the poet's methods.	comments on some of the poet's methods, and their effects.	clearly explains the poet's key methods, and their effects.	examines the poet's methods, and their effects.	analyses the poet's methods and how these influence the reader.
	Subject terminology	uses some subject terminology.	uses some relevant subject terminology.	helpfully uses relevant subject terminology.	uses relevant subject terminology effectively.	uses subject terminology to make points precise and convincing.

NAIL IT!

- Always focus on the criteria for the band *above* the one you are aiming for.
- Aiming high – but not too high – is a reliable way of hitting – or even exceeding – your target

Write your answer

Sticking to a coherent plan is the best way to write a good answer.

The section 'Unseen poetry: comparing poem pairs' (pages 24–55) takes you step by step through some modelled examples of answers. The aim of this page is to give some general advice that you can use for any answer you write.

Give your AQA markers what they want

Know and understand the mark scheme on page 18, especially the descriptors for the level you are aiming for. You will find some examples of writing at different levels in the section 'Unseen poetry: comparing poem pairs' (pages 24–55).

Here are some of the general things that examiners will want to see in your answer, and some tips on how to give them what they want.

What examiners want to see	Explanation	Useful sentence stems
Engage sensitively with the poem. Show your understanding.	Make interesting comments about details. Don't be afraid to say what you find interesting.	I wonder if… That made me feel…
Support your ideas with evidence and examples.	Choose and explore details that are relevant to the poem and the question.	For example,… The phrase '[…]' implies…
Be sensitive to mood and tone.	Tone is the poet's attitude, for example, sad, admiring, mocking.	The tone/mood of the poem is…
Explore imagery and its effects.	Ask yourself how descriptions, similes and metaphors contribute to the poem's mood and meaning.	This image suggests/ shows/makes us feel that…
Stick with what's in the poem.	Don't guess information, such as whether the poem is autobiographical, and don't use a poem's theme as a platform to air your own views about a topic. Stick to exploring the poem in front of you.	The speaker obviously feels… We know this because…
Make *relevant* points about structure and form.	Notice rhythm and rhyme or other ways in which the poem is organised. Suggest how these features affect mood and meaning.	The regular rhythm is appropriate to… Each stanza moves the speaker's point of view one step forward…
Comment on methods the poet used on purpose to make meaning.	Choose three or four key methods. Don't try to write about everything. Use the poet's name to remind yourself that the poem is deliberately created for effect.	[Poet's name]'s repetition of [word] confirms our impression that…

Answering question 2

The second Unseen poetry question is worth eight marks. Leave 15 minutes for it. The question will ask you to compare another poem with the first poem, in terms of the *ways* the poets present their feelings or attitudes. This second poem will also be printed on your exam paper.

Read the poem in light of the question

The advice about reading the first poem mainly applies to the second poem too. The only difference is that you have much less time for the second question, so it is a good idea to read the question *before* you read the second poem. That way you will know what to look out for.

Below is an AQA exam-style question. The question has been prepared by a student so that they fully understand it. Look at their notes.

Underline key, relevant details in the poem.

Poets' methods – form v. different, almost opposite.

AQA exam-style question

In both 'The Eagle' and 'Bat' the speakers describe feelings about an animal. What are the similarities and/or differences between the ways the poets present those feelings?

Eagle/bat

And/or – big contrast but both suggest fear.

Poets' feelings about the animals.

This question is about 'The Eagle' (page 11) that you have already read, and an extract from 'Bat' by D.H. Lawrence (see below). **The poems in your exam will be longer**.

Notice how this student's notes on the poem focus only on *relevant* comparisons with 'The Eagle':

Bat

Wings like bits of umbrella.

Bats!

Creatures that hang themselves up like an old rag, to sleep;
And disgustingly upside down.

Hanging upside down like rows of disgusting old rags
And grinning in their sleep.
Bats!

In China the bat is symbol for happiness.

Not for me!

Just 'Bat', not 'The Bat'.
Less respect than for 'The Eagle'.
Suggests attitude of disgust.

Much more offhand, insulting. Umbrella here is broken man-made thing. Simile in 'Eagle' like thunderbolt'. Majestic, awesome.

Exclamation mark sounds like warning, but disgust.

Ragged, uneven, free verse. Gives no majesty to the bats - cf calm, even verse of 'Eagle'.

Describing words/similes make bats sound like 'down-and-outs'; dirty, not noble.

Rejection of bats.

Plan your answer

The student who wrote the notes on page 20 is obviously a fast worker. However, note that they are reading 'Bat' only in light of its similarities and differences with 'The Eagle'. They do not waste time on irrelevant aspects of the poem. Your quick notes on the second poem are all the planning you will need – or have time for.

Know what your AQA examiner is looking for

AQA will mark your second unseen poetry answer against just one assessment objective (AO2) with a focus on comparing the poets' methods and *how* they affect meaning.

Write your answer

You've made a few relevant notes. Now just answer the question. Keep comparing the two poems. Identify the poets' different (or/and similar) attitudes or feelings and explore some methods the poets have used to present these. It's OK to repeat points you have already made about the first poem in order to make comparisons with the second poem.

Mark scheme

AQA will mark your answers in 'bands'. These roughly equate as follows:

- band 4 approx. grades 7–9
- band 3 approx. grades 4–6
- band 2 approx. grade 3
- band 1 approx. grades 1 and 2.

The improvement descriptors below will help you understand how to improve your answer and, therefore, gain higher marks.

NAILIT!

- Spend up to five minutes reading the second poem and preparing your answer to your exam question.
- Choose three or four key methods to focus on. Don't try to write about everything.

Below is another question on the two poems. Prepare it in the same way as above.

In both 'The Eagle' and 'Bat' the speakers describe their attitudes towards nature. What are the similarities and/or differences between the ways the poets present these attitudes?

Assessment objective (AO)		Improvement descriptors			
		Band 1 Your answer…	**Band 2** Your answer…	**Band 3** Your answer…	**Band 4** Your answer…
AO2 (12 marks)	**Language, form and structure**	makes a couple of links between: – the poets' use of language or structure or form – the effects of those methods.	makes relevant comparisons between: – the poets' use of language and/or structure and/or form – the effects of those methods.	makes detailed and thoughtful comparisons between: – the poets' use of language and/or structure and/or form – the effects of those methods.	explores and compares: – the poets' use of language, structure and form – the effects of those methods.
	Subject terminology	uses some subject terminology.	uses some relevant subject terminology.	uses relevant subject terminology effectively to support comparisons.	uses subject terminology to make comparisons precise and convincing.

Going for the top grades

Of course you will always try to write your best answer possible, but if you are aiming for the top grades, then it is vital to be clear about what your examiner will be looking out for.

A great answer **will not** waste words or use evidence or subject terminology for its own sake.

A great answer **will** show that you are engaging directly and thoughtfully with the poems and the question, not just writing about the poems according to a formula or 'tick list' you have learned by heart.

The best answers will be **RIPE** with ideas and engagement:

R	• Relevant	Stay strictly relevant to your exam questions.
I	• Insightful	Develop relevant insights into the poems, their **language** and themes, and their tones. You need to take a conceptual approach to the poems. That means establishing a thoughtful point of view at the start, and developing it during the rest of your answer. Here is the opening of one student's answer to the question about how the poet presents the speaker's attitudes to the eagle's power in 'The Eagle': The speaker presents the eagle's power as brutal, something he uses suddenly, perhaps randomly, 'like a thunderbolt'. The poem makes the eagle sound like a tyrant, yet the speaker's presentation of this power is admiring with a suggestion of willing surrender. This is a very disturbing attitude to power. Clearly this answer will not just identify the speaker's attitudes and point out some of the ways those attitudes are expressed: it will also argue and support a particular interpretation – that Tennyson's attitude to power is admiring and 'with a suggestion of willing surrender' that has disturbing implications. This answer is taking an original, *conceptual* approach to the exam question.
P	• Precise	Choose and use evidence precisely so that it strengthens your points and makes them very clear and convincing.
E	• Exploratory	*Explore* relevant aspects of the poems, looking at them from more than one angle. Top answers will often use words and phrases that keep the possibility of alternatives open, so that meaning and effect can be explored, not just stated, such as: • This *might* mean/imply/show… • *Perhaps* the poet meant us to think that… • *Although… on the other hand…*

Language, structure and form

The top band in the mark scheme makes it clear that when you compare the *ways* the poets create tone and attitude, you must refer to language, structure *and* form.

Subject terminology

Some students who are aiming high try to show off their knowledge of subject terminology, littering their answers with impressive words such as 'litotes', 'caesura', '**trochaic meter**', and so on. Subject terminology is only relevant if it supports points and makes them clearer. Well chosen, well used subject terminology will do just that. Irrelevant subject terminology will simply confuse and blur meaning.

STRETCHIT!

Write a RIPE opening for this exam question:

In both 'The Eagle' and 'Bat' the speakers describe their attitudes towards nature. What are the similarities and/or differences between the ways the poets present these attitudes?

Tip: Try to establish a clear, conceptual point of view at the beginning of your answer.

REVIEW IT!

1   In your exam, how long should you give yourself to prepare, plan and write your Unseen poetry question 1 answer?

2   In your exam, how long should you give yourself to prepare, plan and write your Unseen poetry question 2 answer?

3   How long should you spend planning and preparing each of the two Unseen poetry answers?

4   Why is it important to prepare your exam question carefully?

5   If you are in your exam and you find that you can't identify one fixed meaning in the poem, what can you do?

6   Why might it be helpful to keep a list of prompts in mind as you approach the unseen poems?

7   What will be the key focus for the Unseen poetry question 2?

8   Create your own question by filling in the blanks in response to any of the poem pairings in this guide:
In [name of poem] how does the poet present [the speaker's feelings about/ attitudes to/the effects of] [poem's theme/focus]?

9   Create your own question by filling in the blanks in response to any of the poem pairings in this guide:
In both [poem 2] and [poem 1] [the speakers] describe [their attitudes to/ feelings about] [focus/theme common to both poems]. What are the similarities and/or differences between the ways the poets present [those/ these] [feelings/attitudes]?

10 Plan an answer to the question you created in question 8 above.

AQA Unseen poetry – comparing poem pairs

In the following pages we model a step-by-step method of approaching the Unseen poetry questions. There are four pairs of Unseen poems with an example AQA exam-style question at the end of each poem. Each example question is worked through in this section. We also provide AQA exam-style questions for you to answer. These are set in yellow boxes.

For each pair of poems we will show you how to:

• interpret the poems by using the response framework

• deal with uncertainty

• write answers to both of the Unseen poetry questions.

You will see examples of exam answers with comments that show how the mark scheme is applied.

As you work through the four pairs of poems, you will see how to develop your understanding while trusting your own judgement and answering the exam questions confidently.

	Pair	Poem 1	Poem 2	Focus
Pages 24–31	1	'Digging' by Edward Thomas	compared with 'Colour Blind' by Lemn Sissay	Using the response framework to explore the poem Using your framework notes to begin your answer to questions 1 and 2
Pages 32–38	2	'The Deserted House' by Alfred Lord Tennyson	compared with 'Living Space' by Imtiaz Dharker	Becoming more confident by using elements of the response framework to explore the poems Dealing with uncertainty: how to write about a poem if you are unsure of the poem's meaning Developing ideas from question 1 to answer question 2
Pages 39–46	3	'I Am!' by John Clare	compared with 'Woman Work' by Maya Angelou	Step-by-step approaches to planning and writing your answers and using the examiner's notes and mark scheme to help you
Pages 47–55	4	'Piano' by DH Lawrence	compared with 'In Between Days' by Raman Mundair	Going for the top grades Making sense of the mark scheme

Pair 1: poem 1

Digging

1 Today I think
  Only with scents, – scents dead leaves yield,
  And bracken, and wild carrot's seed,
  And the square mustard field;

5 Odours that rise
  When the spade wounds the roots of tree,
  Rose, currant, raspberry, or goutweed,
  Rhubarb or celery;

  The smoke's smell, too,
10 Flowing from where a bonfire burns
  The dead, the waste, the dangerous,
  And all to sweetness turns.

  It is enough
  To smell, to crumble the dark earth,
15 While the robin sings over again
  Sad songs of Autumn mirth.

Edward Thomas

Example AQA exam-style question

In 'Digging', how does the poet present the
speaker's attitudes to the smells of autumn?

[24 marks]

DEFINEIT!

bracken – a tall sweet-smelling plant that can cover large areas

goutweed – sweet-smelling plant

mirth – laughing with cheerfulness or amusement

mustard – yellow–flowered plant; the seeds are used to make mustard for the table

odours – smells

yield – natural or agricultural produce

NAIL IT!

- The first Unseen poetry question is worth 24 marks.

- Spend 35 minutes on it.

In your exam it is unlikely that words will be defined for you. However, AQA will give you a poem that does not contain many unusual words.

These pages will show you how to use the response framework with its set of prompts to explore two unseen poems step by step. This is the type of preparation that you could do at the start of your revision for this paper. We will also explore how to begin your answer to the question.

Read the poem

Read 'Digging' calmly and carefully. Notice the title. Try to grasp the basic topic of the poem and perhaps the overall tone.

Understand the question

Read the question carefully before you begin to look for details in the poem. Here a student has prepared the question, to ensure that they fully understand it:

Underline key, relevant details in the poem.

Wonder/curiosity/ happiness/delight?

Poet's methods

Focus on smells of autumn.

Example AQA exam-style question

In 'Digging', how does the poet present the speaker's attitudes to the smells of autumn?

Read the poem again

Explore the poem, referring to the prompts in the response framework (see page 13) and keeping the focus of the exam question in mind. Focus on the **methods** the poet uses and underline and annotate details in the poem that will help you answer the exam question.

Let's go back over the poem, using the response framework to help us:

1	**What do I notice about the exam question?**
	The question asks me to look at the methods the poet uses to present attitudes to the smells of autumn.

2	**What is the poem about?**
	The speaker's attitude to the smells of autumn is the pleasure that can be achieved by the simple act of focusing on this sense of smell – thinking 'Only with scents'.

3	**What do I notice about the title of the poem?**
	The title refers to the ordinary and manual task of digging. This may not seem an especially pleasurable or poetic attitude, but we know from the question that there is a focus on the sense of smell, so we can imagine the smells that could be linked with digging in a garden.

4	**What do I notice about the poem's tone or mood?**
	The poem seems to have a mood of contentment and pleasure. The speaker is going to focus on thinking 'Only with scents'. This mood suits the simplicity of the physical act of digging and the speaker's attitude of wonder and immersion in the 'Odours that rise'.

DO IT!

Remind yourself of the response framework on page 13. Underline five key relevant details in 'Digging'.

5 **What do I notice about the poem's form?**
The speaker's attitude towards the simplicity of thinking 'Only with scents' is also seen through the poem's neat form, comprising four, four-lined stanzas with a regular but unusual rhyme scheme where lines 2 and 4 rhyme in each stanza. (It's 'unusual' because it could be argued that 'tree' and 'celery' only nearly rhyme as the 'ry' in 'celery' is unstressed.)

6 **What do I notice about the poem's structure (how it is organised)?**
The opening line of each stanza makes a clear statement. In the first stanza, the narrator tells us that 'Today I think' before developing that idea in the second line, 'Only with scents'. This is decisive and matter of fact in tone. This pattern is used again in the final stanza, where the dramatic statement 'It is enough' continues in the second line, 'To smell'.

Each stanza develops the speaker's focus on the sense of smell as they list fragrant plants and shrubs: 'Rose, currant, raspberry, or goutweed'.

The turning point in this pleasure is introduced at the end of the poem with the introduction of another sense (hearing) with the 'sad songs of Autumn'.

7 **Which lines, phrases or words stand out? Why?**
'When the spade wounds the roots of tree' stands out to me. The speaker is describing the autumnal smells as the spade cuts into the soil. However, the word 'wounds' suggests cuts received through violent conflict. This is at odds with the pleasurable attitude and links with the 'dead, the waste, the dangerous' in the next stanza. This list with its negative attitude is transformed through autumn's bonfires into 'sweetness'.

The contrast in the final line between 'sad songs' of 'Autumn mirth' creates a thoughtful attitude, as if the reader is asked to consider that autumn, with its lush smells, will be followed by the cold and stark winter.

8 **Do I notice any obvious poetic devices (for example, imagery, metaphors, enjambment)? What is their effect?**
The language is simple and direct. The use of monosyllabic words in the opening of each stanza creates an attitude of confidence and sincerity about the statements. The speaker is at one with the natural world and tells us simply, 'This is enough'. The lists of types of plant are used almost like a prayer: '<u>And</u> bracken, <u>and</u> wild carrot seed/<u>And</u> the square mustard field;' through the repeated structure using 'and'.

The use of the active **verbs** 'To smell, to crumble' with this repeated pattern suggests the physical nature of digging. There is a physical sense of taking the soil into our hands as we 'crumble' the 'dark earth' suggesting also the lush nature of the soil. Notice also how the smoke is 'Flowing' – again active and dynamic and an element that could have negative **connotations** and attitudes.

9 **What is the poet trying to say?**
Edward Thomas is saying things on different levels. On the one hand he is describing the physical, literal season of autumn and the activities and experiences in the garden. Additionally, though, he is perhaps commenting on the cyclical nature of the seasons and the passing of time/lifetime, as experienced through the senses.

10 **Is there anything odd or curious in the poem?**
The mix of positive and negative associations is intriguing. The seemingly negative 'dead leaves' yield scents; the spade 'wounds' the roots of the tree; smoke and fire turns the 'waste' and the 'dangerous' to 'sweetness.' Is Thomas suggesting here that everything good will pass – just as autumn will past into winter? Or is he suggesting that even negative elements can turn into sweetness?

 **DO**IT!

Plan your answer

Using the notes here and your own ideas on the poem, create a plan for your answer to the question on page 25. Remember that you should pay particular attention to:

- Thomas's attitudes
- his methods
- the smells of autumn.

 DOIT!

What section of the response framework has the student used to begin their answer?

STRETCHIT!

Complete the opening paragraph to this exam-style question.

Write your answer

Here is one student's opening to their answer:

Refers to the poem's title.

Uses the name of the poet.

In 'Digging', Edward Thomas presents the speaker's attitudes to the smells of autumn as one of contentment and pleasure.

Uses the words from the question.

Directly answers the question showing their understanding of the speaker's attitudes.

Now answer this question:

AQA exam-style question

In 'Digging', how does the poet present the speaker's feelings about nature?

[24 marks]

Pair 1: poem 2

Colour Blind

¹ If you can see the sepia in the sun
  Shades of grey in fading streets
  The radiating bloodshot in a child's eye
  The dark stains on her linen sheets
⁵ If you can see oil separate on water
  The turquoise of leaves on trees
  The reddened flush of your lover's cheeks
  The violet peace of calmed seas

  If you can see the bluest eye
¹⁰ The purple in petals of the rose
  The blue anger, the venom, of the volcano
  The creeping orange of the lava flows
  If you can see the red dust of the famished road
  The white air tight strike of nike's sign
¹⁵ the skin tone of a Lucien Freud
  The colours of his frozen subjects in mime

  If you can see the white mist of the oasis
  The red, white and blue that you defended
  If you can see it all through the blackest pupil
²⁰ The colours stretching the rainbow suspended
  If you can see the breached blue dusk
  And the caramel curls in swirls of tea
  Why do you say you are colour blind when you see me?

Lemn Sissay

Example AQA exam-style question

In both 'Digging' and 'Colour Blind', the speakers describe *their* attitudes to the power of the senses. What are the similarities and/or differences between the ways the poets present these attitudes?

[8 marks]

DEFINEIT!

breached – burst through	**sepia** – red-brown colour
Lucien Freud – a realistic portrait painter	**turquoise** – greeny-blue colour
radiating – spread from a central point	**venom** – poison secreted by animals

Read the poem with the question in mind

Remember you will only have 15 minutes for this eight-mark question. However, it is important that you fully prepare the question to make sure that you understand it.

Below is one student's preparation for this AQA exam-style question:

> Must compare attitudes to power of senses of smell/sight.

> Underline key, relevant details in the poems.

> Poets' attitudes about the senses.

Example AQA exam-style question

In both 'Digging' and 'Colour Blind' the speakers describe *their* attitudes to the power of the senses. What are the similarities and/or differences between the ways the poets present these attitudes?

> Poets' methods – both use a mix of positive and negative images.

> and/or – the key difference is a contrast in tone between the poems.

Plan your answer

Look at one student's notes on the extract from 'Colour Blind' below. Notice how they link all of their ideas to 'Digging' – the first poem (page 25). These relevant notes are the student's plan for an answer.

Colour Blind

If you can see the sepia in the sun
Shades of grey in fading streets
The radiating bloodshot in a child's eye

Inability to see certain colours but the last line suggests the poet is referring to skin colour. Political/angry tone unlike 'Digging', which has a celebratory/joyous tone of pleasure in the senses

Direct and clear statement (accusing in tone?) to start each stanza. Questioning a person's use of the sense of sight. Also a clear and direct statement in 'Digging': 'Today I think'. Not accusing in tone unlike 'Colour Blind', instead making a decision about using the sense of smell to think. There is a tone and sense of pleasure from this decision.

A violent and shocking image suggesting the colour red dramatically. This is especially shocking as it is linked to a 'child', normally associated with protection and comfort. In 'Digging', the 'The dead, the waste, the dangerous' is turned to 'sweetness' - these negatives become positive, a further difference from 'Colour Blind'.

Write your answer

The student refers to the question and immediately begins their answer with a key difference.

The student knows they need to focus on the poets' methods – the 'way' each poet present their attitudes.

The student uses the names of both poets to remind themselves that they must refer to both poems.

> A key difference between the ways Edward Thomas and Lemn Sissay present their attitudes to the senses is through the tone of their poems.

The student immediately refers to 'tone' – one of the methods a poet can use.

NAIL IT!

- Leave just 15 minutes to answer Unseen poetry question 2.
- Once you have made a few notes, immediately begin your answer.
- Make sure that you focus on the writer's methods and keep comparing the two poems.

The next sentences will continue to explore *how* the poet uses tone to show their attitude to the senses – again showing the student's understanding of the poet's methods.

Uses quotations from both poems to support their ideas

Clearly defines the tone of each poem

> Sissay's poem begins with 'if you can see', immediately setting a challenging tone. This use of a direct and clear statement demands that if these colours can be easily seen - easily sensed - then skin colour can also be seen. Thomas's poem also begins with a clear and direct statement, 'Today I think'. However, this reference to using the sense of smell to 'think' is not accusing in tone; instead there is a tone and sense of pleasure from this decision.

Keeps the answer on track through references to the senses, therefore keeping the question in mind

Carefully shows how the methods used are the same before they refer to a difference

DO IT!

Using these notes and your own ideas, write your answer to the question. Try to complete your answer in 15 minutes.

Now answer this question:

AQA exam-style question

In both 'Colour Blind' and 'Digging' the speakers describe feelings about nature. What are the similarities and/or differences between the ways the poets present those feelings?

[8 marks]

Pair 2: poem 1

The Deserted House

1 Life and Thought have gone away
Side by side,
Leaving door and windows wide:
Careless tenants they!

5 All within is dark as night:
In the windows is no light,
And no murmur at the door,
So frequent on its hinge before.

Close the door; the shutters close;
10 Or through the windows we shall see
The nakedness and vacancy
Of the dark deserted house.

Come away: no more of mirth
Is here or merry-making sound.
15 The house was builded of the earth,
And shall fall again to ground.

Come away: for Life and Thought
Here no longer dwell;
But in a city glorious –
20 A great and distant city – have bought
A mansion incorruptible.
Would they could have stayed with us!

Alfred Lord Tennyson

Example AQA exam-style question

In 'The Deserted House', how does the poet present the speaker's feelings about the house?

[24 marks]

DEFINE IT!

dwell – live in a specific place

incorruptible – will not die or decay

shutters – wooden panels on windows that can be closed for security or privacy

tenants – people who live in a house owned by someone else

vacancy – empty space

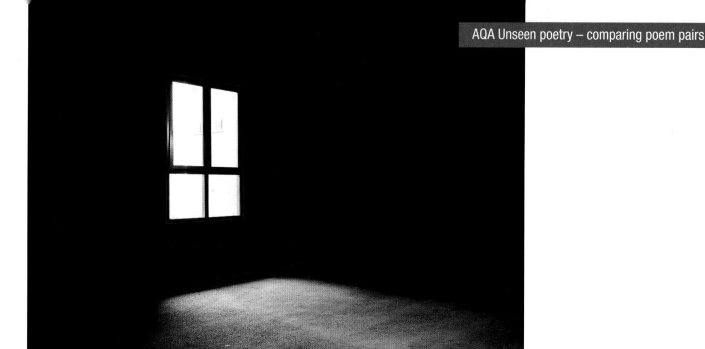

These pages will show you how to use selected elements of the response framework to explore two more unseen poems step by step. We will also explore how to speculate if you are uncertain of a poem's meaning.

Read the question

Think about subject matter and tone.

Here a student has usefully prepared the question, using the response framework:

> 1 What do I notice about the exam question?
>
> The question asks me to look at the *methods the poet uses to present the speaker's feelings about the house.*

Read the poem again

> 2 What is the poem about?

This is where the student is less certain. Here is an extract from their notes:

> The **adjective** 'Deserted' in the title makes me think of feelings of emptiness and absence. We are told that 'light and thought have gone away' - what does this mean? Why are they 'Careless tenants'? Why is there an exclamation mark at the end of 'Careless tenants they!'? Perhaps this suggests that the speaker is angry with the tenants. Why is there a change of tone at the end of the poem? The last line suggests regret.

The student's notes focus on feelings so they are relevant to the exam question. The student has already pinpointed feelings of emptiness, absence, anger and regret, so even though they are uncertain about the poem, they are using their knowledge of the response framework to look at the poem from a number of points of view.

DO IT!

See how this student has used the response framework to guide their analysis of 'The Deserted House'. Note where they have commented on these four prompts in the response framework:

- title
- tone
- language
- structure.

Plan your answer

The student has begun to engage with the methods used by the poet to present the speaker's feelings about the house even though they have not fully grasped the meaning of the poem. Here they use response prompt 10 (Is there anything odd or curious in the poem?) to explore the last two stanzas.

Come away: no more of mirth
Is here or merry-making sound.
The house was builded of the earth,
And shall fall again to ground.

Come away: for Life and Thought
Here no longer dwell,
But in a city glorious -
A great and distant city - have bought
A mansion incorruptible.
Would they could have stayed with us

Repetition. It is an imperative – therefore commanding, but its repetition changes the tone to pleading.

Sounds used again in this stanza to contrast with the feeling of emptiness in the house. Suggests that this house was once a happy place. Why has it changed? Repeated 'm' suggests laughter.

When life and thought are no longer present then perhaps something is dead.

Means will not die or decay. Could this mansion possibly be a metaphor for a body?

Is this referring to someone dying? This would mean that the house was a metaphor for a person dying. It is not just a house.

How to write about a poem if you are uncertain of its meaning

When you read an unseen poem in your AQA exam, don't worry if you don't understand everything. As we showed in the previous pages, stay calm and try to pick up on the general sense and tone of the poem.

If you are in doubt about something, just write, 'this *might* mean...' or '*perhaps*...' or '*seems*…' or '*may*…' Use these sorts of tentative words when writing about details you are unsure about.

Look at how one student explores the final stanza of 'The Deserted House'.

Remember, this is part of an answer to the question:

Example AQA exam-style question

In 'The Deserted House', how does the poet present the speaker's feelings about the house?

Following the speaker's feelings of anger at the 'Careless tenants they!', signalled by the exclamation mark, there is a turning point within the structure and tone of the poem when we reach the final stanza. The tone seems to change with the repetition of 'Come away' as it perhaps becomes less commanding and more pleading. 'Life and thought' no longer live in this house, perhaps suggesting that the house may be seen as a metaphor for a dead body rather than an actual house. This might mean that the whole poem is presenting feelings of grief and regret, instead of merely describing feelings of absence in a deserted house. The structure of the final stanza, with its surprising additional line, seems to support this interpretation of Tennyson's presentation of the speaker's feelings. This disruption of the structure reflects the disruption close relationships face when someone dies. The agony suggested by the pleading tone of 'would they could have stayed with us' confirms our impression that this poem is showing us the reality of grief and loss.

Examines the poet's methods, and their effects.

Uses relevant terminology effectively.

Develops a thoughtful commentary on the poem in relation to the question.

Thoughtfully builds appropriate references into points.

 **STRETCH IT!**

Using this example exam question, write a paragraph about the first two or three stanzas of the poem.

 **DO IT!**

Underline where the student has used tentative language to explore details in the poem that they are unsure of.

Now answer this question:

AQA exam-style question

In 'The Deserted House', how does the poet present the effects of loss?

[24 marks]

Pair 2: poem 2

Living Space

1 There are just not enough
    straight lines. That
    is the problem.
    Nothing is flat
5 or parallel. Beams
    balance crookedly on supports
    thrust off the vertical.
    Nails clutch at open seams.
    The whole structure leans dangerously
10 towards the miraculous.

    Into this rough frame,
    someone has squeezed
    a living space

    and even dared to place
15 these eggs in a wire basket,
    fragile curves of white
    hung out over the dark edge
    of a slanted universe,
    gathering the light
20 into themselves,
    as if they were
    the bright, thin walls of faith.

Imtiaz Dharker

Example AQA exam-style question

In both 'The Deserted House' and 'Living Space', the speakers describe their attitudes towards a place. What are the similarities and/or differences between the ways the poets present these attitudes?

[8 marks]

DEFINEIT!

crookedly – twisted out of shape

miraculous – like a miracle

parallel – surfaces/lines that run side by side with the same distances between them

vertical – upright, straight up

Read the poem with the question in mind

Below is one student's preparation for this AQA-style question. This has allowed them to be clear about what is being asked for when they read the poem.

> ### Example AQA exam-style question
> In both 'The Deserted House' and 'Living Space', the speakers describe their attitudes towards a place. What are the similarities and/or differences between the ways the poets present these attitudes?

Underline key, relevant details in the poems.

Poets' attitudes towards a place.

Must compare attitudes to a place.

Poets' methods – both use of a mix of positive and negative images.

And/or – the key difference is a contrast in tone between the poems.

Know what your AQA examiner is looking for

In this section of your exam paper, remember that you must keep comparing the two poems. For this question, you will need to identify the poets' different and/or similar feelings about a place. To do this, you need to explore some of the methods the poets have used to present their attitudes towards a place.

Below is part of a student's answer. The student is writing about the difference in tone between the poems. Read the comments.

The tone of 'The Deserted House' reflects the speaker's desolate attitude towards this place where 'Life and Thought have gone away.' Tennyson signals this emptiness from the start with 'Deserted' in the title suggesting the place is abandoned with nothing living there. In contrast to the silence of a place with 'no murmur', Dharker presents a place teeming with life. It is a 'Living Space' and the title suggests a double meaning of a house or home as well as a space that is 'Living and alive'.

The tone of Dharker's poem presents a vibrant celebration of a sense of place. Even though there are not enough 'straight lines', which can be seen as a problem, the dangerous lean of the walls is seen as 'miraculous'.

Use of short quotations to support ideas.

Use of words from the question to keep the analysis on track.

Use of the poet's name to show these choices are made on purpose.

Thoughtful comparisons between the effects of the poets' methods.

Explores and compares the poets' use of language.

NAILIT!

AQA will mark your second Unseen poetry answer against just one assessment objective (AO2). This assessment objective focuses on comparing the poets' methods and *how* they affect meaning.

Write your answer

When you write your answer to question 2, remember that you can repeat relevant points you used in your answer to the first question. Make sure you link your points to the second poem.

Below, a student has commented on the structure of the poems. Look how they re-use an idea from their answer to question 1.

Idea from question 1 on 'The Deserted House'	Idea developed for question 2
The structure of the final stanza, with its surprising additional line, seems to support this interpretation of Tennyson's presentation of the speaker's feelings. This disruption of the structure reflects the disruption close relationships face when someone dies.	In Dharker's poem, 'Living Space', the structure is as crazy as the buildings she is describing. The 'Beams' that 'balance crookedly' are represented through the use of enjambement splitting this image across two lines so that it too is balanced. Although the poem is written using short lines, we are told that that the 'The whole structure leans dangerously' with the final word itself 'dangerously' taking up space beyond the edge of the poem. In a similar way Tennyson's disruption of the neat four-lined stanzas by including an additional final line, allows the reader to feel the disruption of the agony of loss and grief. The final line, 'would they could have stayed with us', provides a turning point as we realise that this poem is not merely a poem about a house, but is about the world, the place when someone dies.

DO IT!

Write up to 100 words to continue this response to the question.

Now answer this question:

AQA exam-style question

In both 'The Deserted House' and 'Living Space', the speakers describe their feelings about the idea of home. What are the similarities and/or differences between the ways the poets present those feelings?

[8 marks]

Pair 3: poem 1

I Am!

1 I am—yet what I am none cares or knows;
  My friends forsake me like a memory lost:
  I am the self-consumer of my woes—
  They rise and vanish in oblivious host,
5 Like shadows in love's frenzied stifled throes
  And yet I am, and live—like vapours tossed

  Into the nothingness of scorn and noise,
  Into the living sea of waking dreams,
  Where there is neither sense of life or joys,
10 But the vast shipwreck of my life's esteems;
  Even the dearest that I loved the best
  Are strange—nay, rather, stranger than the rest.

  I long for scenes where man hath never trod
  A place where woman never smiled or wept
15 There to abide with my Creator, God,
  And sleep as I in childhood sweetly slept,
  Untroubling and untroubled where I lie
  The grass below—above the vaulted sky.

John Clare

Example AQA exam-style question

In 'I Am', how does the poet present the speaker's attitudes to being alone?

[24 marks]

DEFINE IT!

abide – stay, live

esteems – things he sees as important

forsake – abandon, leave alone

oblivious – unaware

throes – agonies

vaulted – arched

The pages in this section will show you step by step how to plan and write your answer to the exam question. You will also study some complete sample answers.

Read the poem

Read 'I Am!' calmly and carefully. Notice the title: 'I Am!' Notice the exclamation mark. You will find that the speaker seems very unhappy. In the last stanza they tell us about what they would need in order to be happy again.

DO IT!

Write brief answers to these two prompts from the response framework:

- What is the poem ('I Am!') about?

- What do I notice about the poem's tone or mood?

Understand the question

Make sure you understand the exam question before you plan and write your answer.

Underline key, relevant details in the poems.

Poet's methods

Example AQA exam-style question
In 'I Am!', how does the poet present the speaker's attitudes to being alone?

Self-pitying/resentful/yearning

Being alone/loneliness

Read the poem again with the question in mind

As you read, underline short parts of the poem that seem very relevant to the exam question. Make a few notes next to those lines:

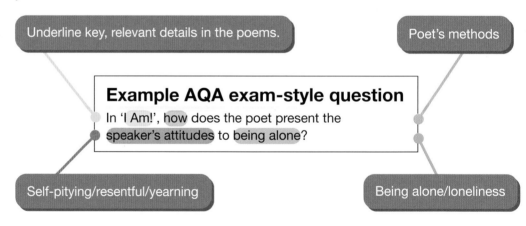

I am—yet what I am <u>none cares</u> or knows;
My friends forsake me like a memory lost:
I am the <u>self-consumer</u> of my woes—

Bit pathetic? No one cares about me; everyone's abandoned me.

Almost as though they enjoy their own 'woes' - self-indulgent? Likes being alone?

40

Plan your answer

Now do a quick outline plan for your answer. There are two main aspects that you need to deal with in your plan:

- the speaker's *attitudes* to being alone ('what')

- the ways in which the poet expresses those attitudes ('how').

For 'I Am!' you could either write about each stanza in turn, or you could write about different attitudes in turn. Whichever approach you choose, make sure you write about the way in which the poet expresses those attitudes ('how'). The plan below combines these two approaches; the numbers in the 'When' column refer to times on the exam-room clock.

What	How	When in your Paper 2 exam (2 hours 15 minutes total)
Introduction	Just answer the question!	10.33
Resentful/bitter (stanza 1)	• Nearly regular rhythm and rhyme • Dramatic word choices	10.35
Despair (stanza 2)	• Metaphors and similes (very abstract)	10.43
Pleased (stanza 3)	• Explore effect of a couple of phrases	10.51
Final comment	How do I feel about the poet's attitudes?	10.58

NAIL IT!

Don't forget:

- the response framework on page 13 is something to hang on to as a guide – especially if you are feeling anxious in your exam

- working through the response framework in relation to the poem and the exam question is a simple way of planning and writing your answer.

Write your answer

Remember that the AQA exam-style question was:

Example AQA exam-style question

In 'I Am!', how does the poet present the speaker's attitudes to being alone?

Below you will find a student's complete answer to the question.

Read the answer and the examiner's notes next to it.

In this poem, the speaker sounds lost and abandoned and very unhappy about it. He seems to blame his friends. I know how he feels because I have had a lot of friendship problems at school and they can make you feel very alone.

In the first stanza he feels very resentful and we know this because he says his 'friends forsake' him. Probably forsake is the sort of word they used then for letting someone down, but it also makes me think of the Bible when Jesus asks God, 'why have you forsaken me?' so being let down here is a much bigger deal. Perhaps he feels that even God has gone off and left him. The first verse is a bit confusing though and it's more confusing with all the dashes and interruptions, but that's right really because it is just like the confusion he is feeling - his feeling of being lost, so it works really well. I think he blames his friends because they don't just go, they 'rise' first - as though they are doing it together - like they've planned it, and then they 'vanish', which means he has no chance of finding them.

However, he does lay it on a bit thick in the next stanza. He becomes very abstract and dramatic with the metaphors of being shipwrecked on a stormy sea coming thick and fast. He does seem to be wallowing in his misery and loneliness. He feels like he is living in 'nothingness' - as though he can't get his bearings at all. All around is 'scorn' - as though people are taking the Mick, and 'noise' that is like a torture to him. In fact his description of being lost at sea is a bit like hell. Perhaps that's why he hinted that God had abandoned him in the first stanza. He sounds even more bitter about being abandoned by his friends and says that it is being ignored by his 'dearest', closest friends that he finds most bitter.

Relevant opening, but it would have been a good idea to use the words 'attitudes to being alone' to 'anchor' the required focus of the answer.

Interesting and shows engagement but not really relevant here.

This suggests an organised approach – one stanza at a time.

Some expression is not precise enough because it is slang and too informal.

Intelligent engagement with words and their implications.

Helpful use of subject terminology.

Recognises development of ideas and imagery.

In a way, the last stanza is a surprise. After moaning on about being let down by his friends he shows a different attitude to being alone. Now he looks forward to being completely alone in a place 'where man hath never trod' - or woman. It's as though he thinks the perfect place would be somewhere that has no meanness or contamination of people, a place where he can be reunited with God. He calls God 'my Creator' almost as though he wants God all to himself, so perhaps in the end he is selfish and a bit self-indulgent in his attitude to being alone.

Overall, the poem moves in steps, stanza by stanza. The first one is a bit 'woe is me...they've all gone off and left me'. The next one is this is all torment and a nightmare (or daymare!). The last one is a surprise: he wants to be on his own in a perfect, unspoilt and safe place. The poem mostly rhymes and has ten syllables in each line.

Side notes:

Clearly establishes interesting focus of paragraph

Neat use of quotation and recognises nuances in word choice

Tentative language –'perhaps' –

This is true but does not help appreciation of the poem's ideas. It is not relevant therefore.

Overall comment

This is an engaged and intelligent response. It is organised in a straightforward, chronological way and makes some useful – occasionally perceptive – observations of the effects of language choices. Some closer examination of language choices would have been welcome.

DO IT!

Compare this answer with the mark scheme on page 18.

Which band does the answer best fit? Briefly explain why.

STRETCH IT!

Add some comments to the notes next to the above answer. Choose details in the answer that have not yet been commented on.

In no more than 100 words, explain how the answer could be improved.

Now answer this question:

AQA exam-style question

In 'I Am!', how does the poet present the speaker's feelings about friends?

[24 marks]

Pair 3: poem 2

Woman Work

1 I've got the children to tend
  The clothes to mend
  The floor to mop
  The food to shop
5 Then the chicken to fry
  The baby to dry
  I got company to feed
  The garden to weed
  I've got shirts to press
10 The tots to dress
  The cane to be cut
  I gotta clean up this hut
  Then see about the sick
  And the cotton to pick.

15 Shine on me, sunshine
  Rain on me, rain
  Fall softly, dewdrops
  And cool my brow again.

  Storm, blow me from here
20 With your fiercest wind
  Let me float across the sky
  'Til I can rest again.

  Fall gently, snowflakes
  Cover me with white
25 Cold icy kisses and
  Let me rest tonight.

  Sun, rain, curving sky
  Mountain, oceans, leaf and stone
  Star shine, moon glow
30 You're all that I can call my own.

Maya Angelou

DEFINE IT!

cane – sugar cane; a tall grass used to produce raw sugar

press – to iron

tend – look after

tots – small children

Example AQA exam-style question

In both 'Woman Work' and 'I Am!', the speakers describe their attitudes to their own lives. What are the similarities and/or differences between the ways the poets present these attitudes?

[8 marks]

Read the poem in light of the question

Don't forget to read the question carefully so that you're clear about what to look for In the second poem.

> ## Example AQA exam-style question
>
> In both 'Woman Work' and 'I Am!' the speakers describe their attitudes to their own lives. What are the similarities and/or differences between the ways the poets present these attitudes?

Plan your answer

See how these notes on the poem, 'Woman Work', point out links to the first poem, 'I Am!'.

I've got the children to tend
The clothes to mend
The floor to mop
The food to shop
Then the chicken to fry
The baby to dry
I got company to feed
The garden to weed
I've got shirts to press
The tots to dress
The can to be cut
I gotta clean up this hut
Then see about the sick
And the cotton to pick.

Shine on me, sunshine
Rain on me, rain
Fall softly, dewdrops
And cool my brow again…

Sounds weary, fed up. Short, repetitive lines, matches the woman's repetitive life - Clare uses the same structure for the same reason in I Am!'. Angelou lists these dreary, dreadful jobs that trap her. Are both speakers trapped? In I Am!' the speaker is trapped in his world of 'noise'. Speakers have no control over their lives?

Sounds like a prayer. Why does the speaker use the imperative? Does this show how anxious they are to escape? Clear link to I Am!'.

The notes above are designed to show how to think carefully about a poem. In your actual exam you will not have time to write extensive notes on the poem, but you do need to make notes that help you to think and to notice details. Here are some abbreviated notes a student made on the last four lines of the poem:

Sun, rain, curving sky
Mountain, oceans, leaf and stone
Star shine, moon glow
You're all that I can call my own

Like a church ceiling...cf Clare's 'vaulted sky'.

wants a place of her own - cf speaker in I Am!'

NAIL IT!

- Leave 15 minutes for the second Unseen poetry question.

- Spend up to five minutes reading the poem and preparing your answer.

- Practise this so that you can work *quickly* and *carefully* in your exam.

Write your answer

Below, you will find a student's complete answer to the question.

Read the answer and the notes next to it.

Both of the poems show people left on their own: one is trapped by her continuous work while the other is trapped in a torment of 'scorn and noise' and 'waking dreams'. Both speakers seem to be in a hell that has been made for them. They both use continuous language to express this continuous life that keeps moving so that they can't escape. 'Woman Work' uses short lines and rhymes to give a repetitive feel. 'I Am!' uses long sentences that are not tightly organised to suggest the lack of control the speaker feels about their own life.

Also, both poems suggest what the speakers really want: escape. The speaker in 'I Am!' definitely wants to be with their God - 'my Creator', but 'Woman Work' also has a religious feel. Sometimes it sounds like a prayer because she calls on nature to save her: 'Shine on me, sunshine/ Rain on me, rain', etc. She asks the wind to blow her to a place where she can rest. She also says the 'curving sky' is something she can call her own just as the speaker in 'I Am!' looks forward to being alone and peaceful under 'the vaulted sky'. Both of these remind me of church roofs - looking up at them.

Some observations of methods, but not explained (for example, what is 'continuous language'?).

A number of insights into how the form of poems helps their mood and meaning.

Close observations of similar details gives rise to sensitive interpretation.

Overall comment

This response contains thoughtful comparisons throughout; they are always relevant to the question focus.

Now answer this question:

AQA exam-style question

In both 'Woman Work' and 'I Am!', the speakers describe feelings about what they want. What are the similarities and/or differences between the ways the poets present those feelings?

[8 marks]

Pair 4: poem 1

Piano

1 Softly, in the dusk, a woman is singing to me;
Taking me back down the vista of years, till I see
A child sitting under the piano, in the boom of the tingling strings
And pressing the small, poised feet of a mother who smiles as she sings.

5 In spite of myself, the insidious mastery of song
Betrays me back, till the heart of me weeps to belong
To the old Sunday evenings at home, with winter outside
And hymns in the cosy parlour, the tinkling piano our guide.

So now it is vain for the singer to burst into clamour
10 With the great black piano appassionato. The glamour
Of childish days is upon me, my manhood is cast
Down in the flood of remembrance, I weep like a child for the past.

DH Lawrence

Example AQA exam-style question

In 'Piano', how does the poet present the speaker's feelings about the past?

[24 marks]

DEFINE IT!

appassionato – full of emotion

insidious – sly, sneaky

vista – a long, narrow view

For the final pair of poems in this section, we are going to look at how to aim for the top grades in your exam.

Read the poem

Read the poem, 'Piano', calmly and carefully. Prompts in the response framework may well help you get an overall feeling for the poem and its subject matter. For example:

- What is the poem about?

- What do I notice about the title of the poem?

- What do I notice about the poem's tone or mood?

Understand the question

By now you will realise that AQA Unseen poetry exam questions follow a formula. Even so, you must make sure you understand the question on the paper.

The question you have been asked is:

Example AQA exam-style question

In 'Piano', how does the poet present the speaker's feelings about the past?

This exam question focuses on:

- the speaker's *feelings* about the past

- the *methods* the poet uses to show those feelings.

NAIL**IT!**

Read and study the unseen poems with your exam question focus at the front of your mind.

Read the poem again with the question in mind

You can now look at the poem more closely, noticing *how* the speaker shows his feelings about the past. Look out for methods the poet deliberately uses to affect the reader and to express the poem's meaning.

STRETCH IT!

This response framework grid is partly filled in. Complete the blank sections with your own ideas about 'Piano'.

1	What do I notice about the **exam question**?	
2	What is the poem **about**?	Childhood memories
3	What do I notice about the **title** of the poem?	It doesn't label what the poem is about. The piano is just a trigger for the speaker's nostalgia.
4	What do I notice about the poem's **tone** or **mood**?	
5	What do I notice about the poem's **form**?	Three, four line stanzas, but although there is a regular rhyme scheme (AABB), the lines are different lengths and the frequent enjambement stops the reader emphasising the rhymes. Sometimes parts of lines fall into a rhythm of dee, dee, **dum**.
6	What do I notice about the poem's **structure**? (How is it organised?)	Stanza 1: the speaker is an adult listening to a woman singing. This experience reminds him of a similar childhood experience and his feelings then. Stanza 2:
7	Which **lines**, **phrases** or **words** stand out? Why?	
8	Do I notice any obvious **poetic devices**? What is their **effect**?	
9	What is the poet trying to **say**?	
10	Is there anything odd or **curious** in the poem?	

You will not have time in your exam to carry out such a detailed analysis of the poem. The purpose of the exercise here is to get you to use the response framework to deepen your thinking about an unseen poem in relation to your exam question focus.

NAIL IT!

With some poems and some exam questions you may find that working through the poem stanza by stanza is the best approach, especially if the poet has an idea or mood that they develop from the beginning to the end of the poem. This is probably true of 'Piano' where the poet begins stanzas two and three with phrases that suggest the beginning of a new step in his 'argument' ('In spite of myself...'/'So now...').

Plan your answer

In this section, you have already looked carefully at how to plan and write your answer. You should be much clearer now about how to organise your answer effectively, so here we are going to concentrate on what you need to do to make sure your answer is not just good, but great.

You could use a table like the one below to bring together both the poet's ideas *and* his methods. A couple of suggestions have been offered as examples, but feel free to use your own ideas instead. The 'When' column refers to times on the exam-room clock.

Subtopic	What	How	When in your Paper 2 exam (2 hours 15 minutes total)
	Introduction	Establish a 'conceptual approach' (see page 51)	10.33
1	Stanza 1: 'taken back' to past but detached - sees himself as 'a child'	Explore 'vista' (narrow view) and significance of 'small' (mother fragile?)	10.35
2		'Boom'/'tingling' onomatopoeia - sound is direct and physical	10.43
3			10.51
	Final comment		10.58

 STRETCH IT!

Write a quick plan for your answer.

- Use the planning methods you have practised in this section.

- Make sure you keep the question focus in mind.

Write your answer

Once you have understood the question and the poem, all you have to do is write the answer!

Before carrying on with this section, go back to pages 22–23 and remind yourself of the general advice on top-grade answers.

Your introduction

In a top-grade answer, the introduction is crucial. You need to establish your own intelligent 'take' on the poem – what AQA calls a 'conceptual approach'. For example, a standard answer to our exam question might base itself on the observation that the speaker is longing to return to the safety and security of the past. He has been taken over by a warm sense of nostalgia.

Here, though, is the opening of an answer that shows greater insight into the mood and meaning of the poem:

> At first the speaker only remembers the past, seeing it vividly in his mind's eye. Soon though, this memory overwhelms him so that he feels as though he is travelling back not just into the past, but into the safety and simplicity of his childhood. The speaker is not just yearning for the past, but is also yearning to escape adulthood where he implies that he doesn't get the sense of 'belonging' that he enjoyed as a child.

We might all – from time to time – yearn to go back in time, but this answer suggests there is something more in this poem: the central 'concept' (or idea) that this student is going to explore is that the poem is about the pain of adult life and how this is expressed in a yearning to go back to childhood.

Know what your AQA examiner is looking for

For a top-grade answer, examiners will be looking for evidence that you:

- critically and conceptually **explore** the poem in relation to the question

- choose **precise details** from the poem to make points convincing

- analyse the **poet's methods**, and how these influence the reader

- use **subject terminology** to make points precise and convincing.

 STRETCH IT!

Write your own brief introduction that establishes a conceptual approach, either to the question you have been working on, or to this new question:

> In 'Piano', how does the poet present the effects of memory and nostalgia?

The best way to understand what these criteria mean is to see them in action in an answer. Below is part of one student's answer to the question you have been preparing. Read the answer and the notes alongside.

Although in the first stanza the speaker is able to resist the power of the past, remaining detached from himself as 'a child', in the second stanza he begins to be overwhelmed by his feelings. The effect of the music is an 'insidious mastery'. This is a personification. The phrase suggests the way the music creeps up on him and sneakily takes over his thoughts and feelings so that he cannot consciously resist it. Perhaps 'insidious' also suggests he resents the way the music works on him as though it is unfair in not giving him a proper chance to defend himself. This idea of unfairness is reinforced by the idea that the music 'betrays' him by drawing him back to his past. Perhaps he feels that...

Precise choice of details, with convincing comments on what those details imply.

Pointless mention of subject terminology.

Perhaps/suggest support an open exploratory interpretation.

Some appreciation of how the poet uses deliberate techniques (for example, 'reinforcement') to guide the reader's reaction.

Overall comment

This is an intelligent, exploratory approach that supports insights into the poem with well-chosen details. The student does comment on how specific techniques affect the reader, but this is an underdeveloped aspect of the answer.

Subject terminology and the poet's methods

Below are two extracts from another student's answer to the same question. See how this student uses subject terminology (underlined) to comment on how the poet's methods affect the reader:

The **sibilance** in the first line has a soothing, hushing effect which allows the reader to share the speaker's feelings of being entranced by the music.

The poem includes some complex ideas and phrases but the simplicity and regularity of the rhyme scheme helps to draw the reader through the poem's 'argument', similar to how the speaker feels himself being drawn back through his past.

AQA exam-style question

In 'Piano', how does the poet present the effects of memory?

[24 marks]

Pair 4: poem 2

In Between Days

1 In between the days
 I am waiting
 for the rain to stop,
 the fruit in my kitchen ripens,
5 then rots. While the clothes
 in my wardrobe
 wait for me to lose
 weight. The novel
 inside me waits, while I
10 try to unblock
 my fear. The womb
 waits to be filled.
 My insomniac self waits
 for sleep to come.
15 In between days
 waiting,
 buses arrive,
 planes take off;
 summer comes and fades.

Raman Mundair

Example AQA exam-style question

In both 'In Between Days' and 'Piano', the speakers describe their attitudes to the passing of time. What are the similarities and/or differences between the ways the poets present these attitudes?

[8 marks]

Understand the question

The question on page 53 makes clear that you:

- must compare both poems

- must focus on attitudes to *the passing of time*

- can write about similarities *or* differences in those attitudes (*or* both).

Read the poem with the question in mind

Notice how this student's notes on the end of 'In Between Days' focus on the poet's methods and how these relate to 'Piano' *and* to the exam question focus.

...My insomniac self waits for sleep to come.	Much looser form than in 'Piano' - suggests weariness, depressed? No 'glamour'
In between days waiting,	Simple list of actions, again weary, indifferent, defeated
buses arrive, planes take off; summer comes and fades.	Short lines suggest a quicker passing of time - nothing to hold onto to stop it passing

Plan your answer

Making a few notes on the second poem (as above), picking up on *relevant* similarities and differences with the first poem, is all the planning you will need.

Write your answer: introduction

Try to establish your own intelligent 'take' on the poem – what AQA calls a 'conceptual approach' – as in this opening to one student's answer:

> In 'Piano', the speaker is taken over by an active longing to return to the past that he 'weeps for', suggesting both grief and desperation. By contrast, the speaker in 'In Between Days' is passive and pessimistic, letting time wait for her but then move on without her. The force of time seems to leave her irrelevant on one side, and does not sweep her up as in 'Piano'.

This is an excellent opening because it establishes a clear focus for the rest of the answer: the student can now explain how the poems' different language, form and structure suit their different attitudes towards time passing.

Language, form *and* structure

The top band in the mark scheme makes it clear that when you compare the *ways* the poets create tone and attitude, you must refer to language, form *and* structure.

Know what your AQA examiner is looking for

Because there are only eight marks available for this second Unseen poetry answer, the mark scheme is very specific and narrowly focused. For a top-grade answer, your examiner will be looking for evidence that you:

- explore and compare the poets' use of language, form and structure and the effects of those methods

- use subject terminology to make comparisons precise and convincing.

DO IT!

The form of 'In Between Days' is loose and uncontrolled – lines short but varying in length – and this reflects the speaker's failure even to try to control time, to do anything constructive as it passes. The speaker seems detached and without purpose – just like the poem's form. The structure too is loose, based on repetitions of random and varied facts, only emphasising 'waiting'. The form and structure is slippery – just like how the speaker experiences time passing....

....By contrast, in 'Piano', the speaker claims to lose control over his feelings and even over time, which is 'upon' him as though he is overwhelmed by it, yet the poem's form and structure are quite controlled. The form is three, four-line stanzas with an AABB rhyme scheme. The structure is based on three rational movements: imagining the past, triggered by the music; his failed attempt to stay in the present; his conclusion ('so...') that resistance is futile/his surrender to the past and his grief for its loss. A number of phrases in the poem perhaps suggest that his defeat is almost unfair...

Explores connection between form and meaning/effect on reader.

Helpful signal of comparison between poems.

Precise subject terminology.

Look at the next part of the same student's answer (left).

- Read the answer carefully and note down examples of its strengths.

- Refer to notes on what the examiner will be looking for on this page and the 'RIPE' framework (page 22) to guide your comments.

- Don't forget that this is only part of the student's answer. Other strengths might well be shown in the rest of the answer.

- Three comments have been suggested as examples.

AQA exam-style question

In both 'In Between Days' and 'Piano', the speakers describe feelings about losing control. What are the similarities and/or differences between the ways the poets present those feelings?

[8 marks]

NAIL IT!

To lift your answer towards the top grades you need to:

- be RIPE (relevant, insightful, precise, exploratory)

- meet the criteria for the top band in the mark scheme

- adopt a 'conceptual approach' to the poems.

Essentials

NAIL**IT!**

NAIL**IT!**

- When you use subject terminology, make sure that you show the *effect* of the device on the reader. There are no marks for just spotting features in a poem.

- In question 2, examiners are looking for *comparisons* between the poems. If you make a point about one poem, then compare the other poem on that point.

Know what your AQA examiner is looking for

AQA will mark your answer to question 1 on the first unseen poem according to a mark scheme based on the English literature assessment objectives 1 and 2. There are 12 possible marks for each assessment objective, making a total of 24 marks. Spend 35 minutes on this question.

AO1 will expect you to show evidence that you can read, understand and respond to texts. Therefore, your examiner will be looking for evidence that you can:

- develop an informed personal response about an unseen poem and write about it effectively

- use references to the poems, including quotations, to support your ideas and interpretations.

AO2 will expect you to show evidence that you can:

- analyse the language, form and structure used by a writer on purpose to create meaning or effects

- use relevant subject terminology where appropriate.

AQA will mark your answer to question 2 (where you look at similarities and differences between the two poems) according to a mark scheme based *only* on AO2, therefore you will be focusing on the language, form and structure of the two poems and showing how they are the same or different. There are eight marks available for this question. Spend 15 minutes on this question.

DO**IT!**

1 Look at this extract from a student's answer to question 1 on the sense of place in Imtiaz Dharker's poem, 'Living Space'.

Notice that the answer focuses on the poem's context. Why would this section of the response be awarded **no** marks?

> The poem, 'Living Space', is set in the slums of Mumbai. This is a place that is very hot and crowded. Imitiaz Dharker was born in Pakistan.

2 For question 2 of the paper, a student has run out of time and has written about the second unseen poem only. Why would this answer be awarded **no** marks?

Theme

Your exam question will give you a key focus. This is why it is important to read and prepare the question carefully. Don't lose sight of the question focus. Reading the poem with the question in mind will draw your attention to relevant aspects of the poem, and ensure you do not write about things that have not been asked for.

The poet's methods

Language

When you read your unseen poems, notice any similarities in language style and methods, even if the poems come from different points in history. For example, a poem may use an **extended metaphor** of a battle to show the violence of the sea, or they may use natural imagery to show how a child is growing up.

Other patterns of language you could explore include:

- the creation of a **mood/tone**, **perspective/voice**
- the use/effect of particular **word choices**
- the use/effect of **description** including **imagery**
- **titles**
- **sound patterning**
- **tense**
- **punctuation**.

Structure and form

Think about how the structure and form of each poem supports their meaning and effect. For example, is the structure flowing and delicate or dense and formal? Why does the poet use these structures? What is the effect on the reader?

It is worth 'hearing' the poems as you read them to help you to hear the rhythms and sounds that give poems a distinct pattern and coherence. Some poems are like songs, for example, but you will find that all the poems have their own distinctive sound. Think about how the poet may use lines, words and sounds to drive the pace of the poem or to slow it down. Think about the effects the poet wished to create through these methods.

NAILIT!

Concentrate on the key focus in your exam questions.

Make sure you:

- spot and understand the key focus in the questions
- stay relevant to that focus throughout your answer.

Choose some poems from this *GCSE 9–1 AQA English Unseen Poetry* guide.

- Read them aloud.
- Note down anything distinctive about patterns in them, for example: sounds, rhymes, etc.
- Find and compare other poems that have examples of similar patterns. You might find poems to compare in this book, or in other places.

AQA exam-style questions

On these pages you will find two practice questions for each pair of poems.
Answer both questions.

PAIR 1: PRACTICE QUESTION 1

Catrin

1 I can remember you, child,
  As I stood in a hot, white
  Room at the window watching
  The people and cars taking
5 Turn at the traffic lights.
  I can remember you, our first
  Fierce confrontation, the tight
  Red rope of love which we both
  Fought over. It was a square
10 Environmental blank, disinfected
  Of paintings or toys. I wrote
  All over the walls with my
  Words, coloured the clean squares
  With the wild, tender circles
15 Of our struggle to become
  Separate. We want, we shouted,
  To be two, to be ourselves.

  Neither won nor lost the struggle
  In the glass tank clouded with feelings
20 Which changed us both. Still I am fighting
  You off, as you stand there
  With your straight, strong, long
  Brown hair and your rosy,
  Defiant glare, bringing up
25 From the heart's pool that old rope,
  Tightening about my life,
  Trailing love and conflict,
  As you ask may you skate
  In the dark, for one more hour.

Gillian Clarke

In 'Catrin', how does the poet present the speaker's feelings
about her relationship with her child?

[24 marks]

PAIR 1: PRACTICE QUESTION 2

The Playhouse Key

1   This is the key to the playhouse
    In the woods by the pebbly shore.
    It's winter now, I wonder if
    There's snow about the door?

5   I wonder if the fir trees tap
    Green fingers on the pane,
    If sea gulls cry and the roof is wet
    And tinkle-y with rain?

    I wonder if the flower-sprigged cups
10 And plates sit on their shelf,
    And if my little painted chair
    Is rocking by itself?

Rachel Field

In both 'The Playhouse Key' and 'Catrin', the speakers describe their feelings about childhood. What are the similarities and/ or differences between the ways the poets present those feelings?

[8 marks]

PAIR 2: PRACTICE QUESTION 1

My Grandmother

1 She kept an antique shop – or it kept her.
Among Apostle spoons and Bristol glass,
The faded silks, the heavy furniture,
She watched her own reflection in the brass
5 Salvers and silver bowls, as if to prove
Polish was all, there was no need of love.

And I remember how I once refused
To go out with her, since I was afraid.
It was perhaps a wish not to be used
10 Like antique objects. Though she never said
That she was hurt, I still could feel the guilt
Of that refusal, guessing how she felt.

Later, too frail to keep a shop, she put
All her best things in one narrow room.
15 The place smelt old, of things too long kept shut,
The smell of absences where shadows come
That can't be polished. There was nothing then
To give her own reflection back again.

And when she died I felt no grief at all,
20 Only the guilt of what I once refused.
I walked into her room among the tall
Sideboards and cupboards – things she never used
But needed; and no finger marks were there,
Only the new dust falling through the air.

Elizabeth Jennings

In 'My Grandmother', how does the poet present the speaker's attitudes to her grandmother?

[24 marks]

PAIR 2: PRACTICE QUESTION 2

Childhood

1 I used to think that grown-up people chose
To have stiff backs and wrinkles round their nose,
And veins like small fat snakes on either hand,
On purpose to be grand.
5 Till through the banister I watched one day
My great-aunt Etty's friend who was going away,
And how her onyx beads had come unstrung.
I saw her grope to find them as they rolled;
And then I knew that she was helplessly old,
10 As I was helplessly young.

Frances Cornford

In both 'My Grandmother' and 'Childhood', the speakers describe their attitudes to age. What are the similarities and/or differences between the ways the poets present those attitudes?

[8 marks]

PAIR 3: PRACTICE QUESTION 1

Poem for My Sister

1 My little sister likes to try my shoes,
   to strut in them,
   admire her spindle-thin twelve-year-old legs
   in this season's styles.
5 She says they fit her perfectly,
   but wobbles
   on their high heels, they're
   hard to balance.
   I like to watch my little sister
10 playing hopscotch,
   admire the neat hops-and-skips of her,
   their quick peck,
   never missing their mark, not
   over-stepping the line.
15 She is competent at peever.
   I try to warn my little sister
   about unsuitable shoes,
   point out my own distorted feet, the callouses,
   odd patches of hard skin.
20 I should not like to see her
   in my shoes.
   I wish she could stay
   sure footed,
   sensibly shod.

Liz Lochhead

In 'Poem for My Sister', how does the poet present the speaker's feelings about her little sister?

[24 marks]

PAIR 3: PRACTICE QUESTION 2

Nettles

1 My son aged three fell in the nettle bed.
  'Bed' seemed a curious name for those green spears,
  That regiment of spite behind the shed:
  It was no place for rest. With sobs and tears
5 The boy came seeking comfort and I saw
  White blisters beaded on his tender skin.
  We soothed him till his pain was not so raw.
  At last he offered us a watery grin,
  And then I took my billhook, honed the blade
10 And went outside and slashed in fury with it
  Till not a nettle in that fierce parade
  Stood upright any more. And then I lit
  A funeral pyre to burn the fallen dead,
  But in two weeks the busy sun and rain
15 Had called up tall recruits behind the shed:
  My son would often feel sharp wounds again.

Vernon Scannell

In both 'Poem for My Sister' and 'Nettles', the speakers describe feelings about protecting someone they love.

What are the similarities and/or differences between the ways the poets present those feelings?

[8 marks]

Glossary

adjective A word that describes (or gives more information about) a noun (for example: 'narrow room'; 'stiff backs'; 'sad songs').

alliteration Starting words that are close to each other with the same sound (for example: 'He clasps the crag with crooked hands' in 'The Eagle').

connotation An implied meaning (for example: in 'Catrin', 'that old rope' represents a bond between mother and daughter, but it might also connote something frayed, damaged, discarded; in other words, the image has both positive and negative connotations).

effect The impact that a writer's words have on a reader: the **mood**, feeling or reaction the words create in the reader/viewer.

enjambment Continuing the sense of one line onto the next one. Usually a writer does this by not using punctuation at the end of a line (for example: '...through the windows we shall see/The nakedness and vacancy/Of the dark deserted house, in 'The Deserted House').

extended metaphor A **metaphor** that is reworked and developed in a poem.

form Poems are written in different forms; forms include the technical aspects of poetry, such as sonnet, blank verse, **rhyme**, **stanza**, **rhythm**.

imagery Pictures in words. The main forms of imagery (other than description) are **similes** and **metaphors**.

language The words and the style that a writer chooses in order to have an **effect** on a reader.

metaphor Comparing two things by saying they are the same, for effect (for example: 'the vast shipwreck of my life's esteems' in 'I Am!': his life is not literally a 'vast shipwreck'; it is really just a huge mess).

mood Mood is almost the same as **tone**; it is the atmosphere of a poem, the emotional mood.

personification Treating a thing as though it is alive, a plant or animal as though it is human (for example: 'funeral pyre to burn the fallen dead' in 'Nettles'. The poet treats the nettles as though they are ... who have died in battle).

rhyme A line whose last **stressed** syllable has the same sound as a nearby line ending (for example: eyes/surprise). If the stressed syllable is not the last syllable in a line, then any following syllables must rhyme too (for example: biscuit/risk it).

rhyme scheme The pattern of rhymes in a poem; for example, in each **stanza** you might find that lines 1 and 3 and lines 2 and 4 rhyme. We show this scheme as: ABAB.

rhythm The 'beat' of a line of poetry. Rhythm comes from the way the **stresses** (or 'beats') 'fall', or, more likely, are placed by the poet. If the stresses fall at regular intervals, we say that the line has a 'regular rhythm'.

sibilance A sound effect in which 's' sounds are repeated in words close to each other (for example: 'Softly, in the dusk, a woman is singing' in 'Piano'; 'in the brass/Salvers and silver bowls' in 'My Grandmother').

simile Comparing two things using 'like' or 'as' (for example: 'veins like small fat snakes' in 'Childhood'; 'dark as night' in 'The Deserted House').

stanza Another word for 'verse'. 'Verse' is normally used for songs, 'stanza' for poetry.

stress Emphasis a poet (or reader) places on certain syllables to create a beat or **rhythm** (for example: 'This is the key to the playhouse/In the woods by the pebbly shore' in 'The Playhouse Key').

structure The way a poem is organised so that it is coherent. The structure of a poem is its shape, its patterns of **imagery**, the sequence of its ideas.

tone The attitude of the poet towards what they are writing about. This comes across in their choice of words and **forms**. A tone can change part-way through a poem. Here are some examples of tones: happy, nostalgic, angry, sarcastic, contemptuous, mocking, sad, regretful, longing. There are many others.

trochaic meter A line of poetry which alternates between **stressed** and unstressed syllables, beginning with stressed.

verb A doing, being or having word (for example: to walk, to be or to have). Verbs change their form to show present (walk), past (walked) or future (will walk).